Quotations of Dr. Deming

The Little Blue Book

By
W. Edwards Deming

Sundial Press
Ft. Lauderdale

"We Record The Sunny Hours"

Selected from a variety of sources, these quotations by Dr. Deming appear in this book as part of an on-going effort to spread awareness of the use of statistics and the role of variation in management. Since the purpose of this book is to reach educators, teachers and the people they work with, profits from the sale of this book support distribution of this book to schools, industrial and commercial management and educational leaders. Your purchase of two books allows the publisher to donate another book to a library, a school or a manager in crisis.

Copyright 1994 by Sundial Press
A Division of Future Books/SFEAA
2314 Desota Drive
Ft. Lauderdale, FL 33301-1567
ISBN 1-879857-48-0
First Edition May 1994
Printing 5 4 3 2 1 (read last number)

Acknowledgements

The words and ideas appearing in this book are the property of Dr. W. Edwards Deming. The copyright for the format of this book sits with the Sundial Press. Permission to reprint these words was obtained from Dr. Deming, MIT Center for Advanced Engineering Study, Cecelia Kilian, and Mary Walton.

Introduction

The purpose of this book of quotations is neither to summarize Dr. Deming's work nor to "popularize" his ideas by giving the reader a quick overview. This book does not give you the "essence" of Deming. Rather, the purpose of compiling these quotes is to stir your interest in learning more. Why does Deming advocate the end of merit pay? Why must managers understand terms like "statistical control" and "variation"? You won't find complete answers here, just quotations for you to meditate on and to ponder. The page references will speed your self-education.

Yes, today's world of sound bites, briefings, news summaries and shortened attention spans make Dr. Deming's work hard to communicate to a generation growing up on MTV and to a work force committed to the concepts of intense adversarial competition. Rather than try to chop Deming's philosophy of "managing the system" into 20-second pieces, we have selected quotes that will raise your interest to spend a half-hour or more to learn more about the subject.

The 14 points

We decided to mention just three of Dr. Deming's famous 14 points. If you are moved to find the list of the 14 points and the 7 diseases, then *The Little Blue Book* has achieved its main purpose: to motivate you to read *Out of the Crisis* and other tomes that explain the Deming philosophy of management.

We have not included all of the 14 points and we have omitted the extensive explanations of each point that Deming, his disciples and interpreters have invested many years in developing. This *Little Blue Book* will get you started.

The Editors

The Little Blue Book

Without a cultural revolution in management, quality control circles will not produce the desired effects in America.

> W. Edwards Deming, *Out of the Crisis*, p. 148.

In his foreword to the second edition of *Quotations From Chairman Mao Tse-Tung*, Lin Piao exhorted his readers to "have specific problems in mind, study and apply his [Mao's] works in a creative way, combine study with application." The reader of this little book is encouraged to apply the same advice to Dr. Deming's words.

Students of Chinese history will recall the phrase "cultural revolution" and a certain little **red** book intended to provide the guiding principles for modernizing a country of one billion people. Unlike Deming, whose work empowers those who understand his philosophy, Mao Tse-tung perverted the phrase "cultural revolution" so that those two words continue to revive painful memories in millions of survivors of that ill-conceived plan.

We hope that these quotations from Dr. Deming's work will inspire you to join the larger "cultural revolution" in management. This revolution will change not only you and your neighbors, but also billions of people around the globe, including those who studied Chairman Mao's little red book and failed to find fulfillment. "Peace through economic prosperity" is Dr. Deming's promise to those who heed his call for the pursuit of quality. Let's begin.

The Editors

Table of Contents

Communication

Break down barriers between departments. People in research, design, sales and production must work as a team, to foresee problems of production and in use that may be encountered with the product or service.

Competition

Economists are leading us down the wrong path. They tell us that fierce competition is the solution. We worry about increasing market share and we try to kill off colleagues in the same industry, instead of making better products.

Customers

The customer is the most important part of the production line. Without him, there is no production line. Improvement of quality envelops the entire production line, from incoming materials to the consumer, and redesign of the product and service for the future.

Price has no meaning except in terms of the quality of the product. But that is not enough. Good and uniform quality have no meaning except with reference to the consumer's needs.

Education

I find a general fear of education. People are afraid to take a course. It might not be the right one. My advice is take it. Find the right one later. . . . You never know what could be used, what could be needed. He that thinks he has to be practical is not going to be here very long. Who knows what is practical? Help people to improve. I mean everybody.

Evaluation

Most of us assume that if we don't evaluate you, you won't be motivated to work better. So we interview and measure you, compare you to others, and try to place you in a ranking. Instead we need to promote self-esteem, joy in work and pride in what we do, so that we encourage people innovate and contribute to the job. If we destroy you, you are humiliated. Ranking you destroys you.

Fear

Fear takes a horrible toll. Fear
is all around, robbing people
of their pride, hurting them,
robbing them of a chance to
contribute to the company. It
is unbelievable what happens
when you unloose fear.

Improvement

The only reason to carry out a test is to improve a process, to improve the quality and quantity of the next run or of next year's crop. Important questions in science and industry are how and under what conditions observations may contribute to a rational decision to change or not to change a process to accomplish improvement. A record of observations must accordingly contain all the information that anyone might need in order to make his own prediction.

A company that is healthy, doing well, is in excellent position to improve management, product, and service, thus to contribute to the economic welfare of itself and to the rest of us, and moreover has the greatest obligation to improve. A monopoly is in fact in the best possible position to improve year by year, and has the greatest obligation to do so. A company that is on the rocks can only think of survival.

Putting out fires is not improvement. Finding a point out of control, finding the special cause and removing, is only putting the process back to where it was in the first place. It is not improvement of the process.

We're losing ground because what we are doing is wrong, even though we work very hard and give our best effort.

Joy in Work

I love my work. It's fun for me. I wish American management to keep learning and growing and I wish to keep learning and sharing with them.

When asked why he spends five to seven days per week traveling, teaching, consulting and giving 4-day seminars to hundreds of enthusiastic students, this was Dr. Deming's reply.

Knowledge

Who is it that darkeneth
counsel by words without
knowledge?
(Job 38:2)

My people are destroyed for
lack of knowledge.
(Hosea 4:6)

For in much wisdom is great
grief: and he that increaseth
knowledge increaseth sorrow.
(Ecclesiastes 1:18)

Profound knowledge* of a system comes from outside, rarely from the inside. Have you ever found someone who has profound knowledge *inside* an organization? I never have.

*The understanding needed to improve a system — Editors.

Leadership

Drive out fear, so everyone may work effectively for the company.

Eliminate work standards (quotas) on the factory floor. Substitute leadership.

Eliminate management by objective. Eliminate management by numbers, numerical goals. Abolish the merit system and the ranking of people. Substitute leadership.

Judge each part of a system by its contribution to the system, not for its individual performance. Each part is responsible for the health and well-being of the whole system.

Learning

Learning is not compulsory.
Survival is not compulsory.

Management

My theory of management says that every person gains when the system is optimized.

Management must always improve the system. Do what is best for the *whole* system; don't do things the way they have always been done. Remember: you can't have impact unless you break away from the system, you must be outside of the system.

It is easy to manage a business in an expanding market, and easy to suppose that economic conditions can only grow better and better. In contrast with expectations, we find, on looking back, that we have been on an economic decline for three decades. It is easy to date an earthquake, but not a decline.

The manager should be a leader. He should understand how his work and the work of his people fits into the system. Optimization of a system is the first job of a leader. Recognize that all people are different, try to fit each one in what he does best, what he takes joy in doing.

Most people think of management as a chain of command. My theory says that the system is like an orchestra, not an army. Every one in an orchestra supports the other players. Each player watches not only the conductor, but also each other and the whole system. The system needs a conductor, not a general. It needs someone who harmonizes the talents and abilities of each part of the system. Each player in the orchestra knows he is part of a system, even when he plays solo. He is not there to attract attention to himself. He succeeds when he supports the other players.

Without a cultural revolution in management, quality control circles will not produce the desired effects in America. Nor can anyone guarantee that job security for the rank and file would be enough to produce high productivity and product quality. However, without a management commitment to the personal welfare of its workers, it will be impossible to inspire employees' interest in company productivity and product quality. With guaranteed job security, management's job becomes far more difficult and challenging.

Merit Pay

See **Evaluation.**

Obstacles

Barriers against realization of pride of workmanship may in fact be one of the most important obstacles to reduction of cost and improvement of quality in the United States.

Optimization

Labor and management
should focus on optimizing
the system. For any
discussion between buyer
and seller or suppliers and
retailers, the rule is the same.
If your principal goal in a
negotiation is to protect
yourself, you've already lost –
and so has everyone else.
You gain most when you work
with others to improve the
system.

Any group should have as its aim optimization over time of the larger system that the group operates in. Anything less than optimization of the whole system will bring eventual loss to every component in the system.

Patience

How poor are they that have
not patience.

> Iago to
> Roderigo,
> Shakespeare's
> *Othello,* II, iii.

A Plea For Blood

There are two kinds of blood
in the blood bank, good and
bad. [My physician] Dr.
Burchell used three units of
good blood on me. Bad
blood, he said, is a last
resort.]

People like my friends and
your friends can give good
blood, and that is about the
only source thereof. Blood
from a regular donor that
takes pay for it is almost
dependably pretty well
washed up, like the donor
himself, if I understand Dr.
Burchell correctly.

In other words, good blood comes from friends and from their friends. Money can not buy it: it is not for sale.

I may have garbled some of the medical language here, but Dr. Burchell's point was very clear. He and other surgeons need good blood. Any type will do as replacement.

In short, I owe three pints of good blood, and there is only one way to repay them. Money won't do it. I had not appreciated these critical requirements. Maybe this plea will bring friends to offer blood.

Productivity

Improve constantly and forever the system of production and service, to improve quality and productivity, and thus constantly decrease costs.

Profits

Don't depend on short-term profits as a measure of a system's health. They often don't point to future performance of management. It's easy to report a higher profit by reducing research and postponing maintenance, but the system suffers.

Paper profits do not make the pie bigger. They give you a bigger piece. You take it from somebody else. It doesn't help the society.

Dividends and paper profits, the yardstick by which managers of money and heads of companies are judged, do not improve the competitive position of a company or of American industry. Paper profits do not make bread: improvement of quality and productivity do. They make a contribution to better material living for all people, here and everywhere.

Protectionism

Dependence on protection by tariffs and laws to "buy American" only encourages incompetence.

If some manufacturers in my own country would meet competition with effort, and spend less time on lobbies to boost tariffs and to lower trade quotas, they might have less to worry about Japanese competition and could give some of the rest of us the benefit of better quality and lower prices. Many people say that they believe in free enterprise in competition, but what they often mean is competition for the other fellow, not for themselves.

Now in my own case, I believe in free enterprise, and I am not afraid of Japanese statisticians, English statisticians, French statisticians, or any others. If one of them is doing a better job, then the thing to do is to go over there, or bring him to my own country, and find out how he does it. I don't know of any statistician's lobby to try to keep out foreign statisticians. The more of them we import, the better off we are.

Quality

Why is it that productivity increases as quality improves? Less rework. Not so much waste. Quality to the production worker means that his performance satisfies him, provides to him pride of workmanship.

End the practice of awarding business on the basis of price tag. Instead, minimize total cost. Move toward a single supplier of any one item, on a long-term relationship of loyalty and trust.

Japanese management learned in 1950 . . . that the best solution to improvement of incoming materials is to make a partner of every vendor, and to work together with him on a long-term relationship of loyalty and trust.

Barriers against realization of pride of workmanship may in fact be one of the most important obstacles to reduction of cost and improvement of quality in the United States.

Quality begins at the top. . . . Quality of product and of service can be no better than the intent of top management. The only way a company can achieve success would be for the top management to be committed to the course of action.

Cease dependence on inspection to improve quality. Eliminate the need for inspection on a mass basis by building quality into the product in the first place.

Work with your vendor to improve his incoming quality. Establish a long-term relationship with him for continual improvement, ever better and batter quality, with lower and lower costs. Both you and he will win.

Ranking

See **Evaluation.**

Responsibility

It is no longer socially acceptable to dump employees on to the heap of unemployment. Loss of market and resulting unemployment are not foreordained. They are no inevitable. They are man-made.

The greatest waste in America is failure to use the abilities of people. One need only listen to a tape of a meeting with production workers to learn about their frustrations and about the contribution that they are eager to make. Anyone would be impressed to observe how articulate most production workers are, in spite of criticisms of our schools.

Shewhart, Walter A.
1891-1967

Another half-century may pass before the full spectrum of Dr. Shewhart's contributions has been revealed in liberal education, science, and industry.

Statistics

There are conferences almost any day in this country on the subject of productivity, mostly concerned with gadgets and measures of productivity. As William E. Conway said, measurements of productivity are like accident statistics. They tell you that there is a problem, but they don't do anything about accidents. This book [*Out Of the Crisis*] is an attempt to improve productivity, not just to measure it.

The application of statistical
principles and techniques in
all stages of production
directed toward the economic
manufacture of a product that
is useful and has a market.

A process is in statistical
control when it is no longer
afflicted with special causes.
The performance of a process
that is in statistical control is
predictable.

A professional statistician will not follow methods that are indefensible, merely to please someone, nor to support inferences based on such methods. He ranks his own name and profession as more important than convenient assent to interpretations not warranted by statistical theory. . . . His career as an expert witness will shatter in shipwreck if he indicates concern over which side of the case the results seem to favor. "As a statistician, I couldn't care less," is the right attitude in a legal case, or in any other report.

Most statisticians can recall instances in which informal advice backfired. It is the same in any professional line. A statistician that tries to be a good fellow and give advice under adverse circumstances is in practice and has a client, whether he intended it or not; and he will later on find himself accountable for the advice.

Transformation

Long-term commitment to new learning and new philosophy is required of any management that seeks transformation. The timid and the fainthearted, and people that expect quick results, are doomed to disappointment.

Put everybody in the company to work to accomplish the transformation. The transformation is everybody's job.

Variation

Some leaders forget an important mathematical theorem that if 20 people are engaged on a job, 2 will fall in the bottom ten percent, no matter what. It is difficult to overthrow the law of gravitation and the laws of nature. The important problem is not the bottom 10 percent, but who is statistically out of line and in need of help.

Thousands of people understand that investigation of ups and downs within the control limits creates trouble, increases variation, causes severe loss. These same people forget the basic scientific principles that they have learned [when they go onto] the factory floor; those same scientific principles apply to people. People are the most important asset of any company.

What statistical methods do is to point out the existence of special causes. A point beyond limits on a control chart, or a significant result in an experiment or test, indicates almost certainly the existence of one or more special causes. Points in control, or showing no significance, indicate that only common causes of variation remain.

Management has the obligation to focus attention on common causes of variability and wrong average level. . . . Common causes of variability are often as important as specific causes. Common causes affect all machines and all operators. Only management can change a common cause, the worker can not. No matter how well an operator or a foreman does his work, his efforts may be ineffective if he is handicapped by poor light, raw material that is too variable or otherwise unsuitable, or by any other common cause. This is why management must continually accept the responsibility to find common causes, and to eliminate them if economically feasible.

Work

Anyone with a job is entitled
to pride of workmanship.

Other quotations

Wisdom sounds foolish to fools.

> Dionysius to
> Cadmus in
> Euripedes' *The
> Bacchae.*

Is it the bell that rings,
Is it the hammer that rings,
Or is it the meeting of the two
that rings?

> Japanese poem

Sources

The **boldface** number indicates the page number in this book; the plain number indicates the page number from the source book. For example, **15** 35 means the quote on page 15 is from page 35 of the source book. If there are two quotes on the page, a letter indicates which quotation is being referred to: **16a** is the first quote, **16b** is the second quotation.

The New Economics for Industry, Government, Education. Deming, W. Edwards (1993). MIT Center for Advanced Engineering Study. Quotations: **19** 6, **29** 5, **37** 59

Out of the Crisis. Deming, W. Edwards (1982, 1986). MIT Center for Advanced Engineering Study, 77 Massachusetts Avenue, Room 9-234, Cambridge, Mass. 02139. Order the book through your local book store or contact MIT directly at 617-253-7444. Also available: *The Essential Deming*, a 4-tape video series. Quotations: **12** 24, **22a** 1, **22b** 97, **22c** 371, **24a** 23, **24c** 24, **33** 148, **35** 83, **38** Chapter 2, **41** 23, **43** 21, **44** xi, **47a** 1, **47b** 23, **48a** 43, **48b** 83, **49b** 23, **51** ix, **52** 53, **54** x, **58a** x, **58b** 24, **59** 56, **65a** 486, **65b** 177

The World of W. Edwards Deming. Kilian, Cecelia, S. (1992). Order from SPC Press, 5908 Toole Drive, Suite C, Knoxville, Tenn. 800-545-8602. Quotations: **14a** 24, **14b** 65, **18** 99, **21** 13, **39** 142, **45-46** 43-44, **49a** 22, **50** 10, **53** 88, **55a** 42, **55b** 100, **56** 106, **57** 120, **61** 46, **62-63** 247, **64** 254

The Deming Management Method. Walton, Mary. (1986). Order from Putnam Publishing, 200 Madison Avenue, NY, NY 10016 or from a book store. Quotations: **15** 84, **17** 73, **20a** 67, **42b** 91, **60** 248

All other quotations in this book were made by Dr. Deming in classroom situations.

Some references for your study of Deming's work

The Deming of America, a video series, and a pocket-sized list of the 7 Deadly Diseases and the 14 Points. Produced by Petty Consulting Productions, 229 Oliver Road, Cincinnati, Ohio 45215 (513) 821-9083, fax (513) 821-9708

Dr. Deming: The American Who Taught the Japanese About Quality by Rafael Aguayo, foreword by W. Edwards Deming (1991). Published by Fireside Books, Simon and Schuster, 1230 Avenue of the Americas, New York, NY 10020, ISBN 0-671-74621-9.

If you have a favorite Deming quote that doesn't appear in this book, please send it to the editors at the address given below. Your suggestion will be considered for inclusion in a future edition. If the quote is used, you will receive a free copy of the next edition.

Send your favorite Deming quote to:
Deming Quotes • The Second Edition
Sundial Press, Future Books/SFEAA
2314 Desota Drive
Ft. Lauderdale, FL 33301-1567

To order additional copies of this book, please call 1-800-247-6553 or you can send a check for the amount indicated below. Make the check to: **Bookmasters** and mail to:
Bookmasters Distribution
P.O. Box 2039
Mansfield, OH 44905

Number of books	Cost per book
1	$10 each
2	$9 each
3-5	$8 each
6-10	$7.50 each
10 or more	$6.50 each

Postage will be paid by the publisher on pre-paid orders -- all orders must include a check made to "Bookmasters."

Remember: profits from the sale of this book will allow the publisher to donate copies to schools, libraries and managers in crisis.

Drive out fear.